RIPCORD

OTHER BOOKS BY DAVID LINDSAY-ABAIRE
PUBLISHED BY TCG

Good People

Rabbit Hole

RIPCORD

DAVID LINDSAY-ABAIRE

THEATRE COMMUNICATIONS GROUP
NEW YORK
2017

Ripcord is published by Theatre Communications Group, Inc.,
520 Eighth Avenue, 24th Floor, New York, NY 10018-4156

The publication of *Ripcord* by David Lindsay-Abaire, through TCG's Book Program, is made possible in part by the New York State Council on the Arts with the support of Governor Andrew Cuomo and the New York State Legislature.

TCG books are exclusively distributed to the book trade by Consortium Book Sales and Distribution.

Library of Congress Control Numbers:
2016036069 (print) / 2016044594 (ebook)
ISBN 978-1-55936-519-2 (softcover) / ISBN 978-1-55936-845-2 (ebook)
A catalog record for this book is available from the Library of Congress.

Book design and composition by Lisa Govan
Cover design by Rodrigo Corral Studio / June Park

First Edition, January 2017

RIPCORD

PRODUCTION HISTORY

Ripcord was commissioned by Manhattan Theatre Club through the Bank of America New Play Commissioning Program. It received its world premiere at Manhattan Theatre Club (Lynne Meadow, Artistic Director; Barry Grove, Executive Producer) on October 20, 2015. It was directed by David Hyde Pierce; the set design was by Alexander Dodge, the costume design was by Jennifer Von Mayrhauser, the lighting design was by Peter Kaczorowski, the original music and sound design were by John Gromada, the fight direction was by Thomas Schall; the production stage manager was Denise Yaney. The cast was as follows:

ABBY BINDER	Holland Taylor
MARILYN DUNNE	Marylouise Burke
SCOTTY	Nate Miller
BENJAMIN, LEWIS, CLOWN	Glenn Fitzgerald
COLLEEN, WOMAN IN WHITE	Rachel Dratch
DEREK, ZOMBIE BUTLER, MASKED MAN	Daoud Heidami

CHARACTERS

ABBY BINDER	a resident, seventies–eighties
MARILYN DUNNE	a resident, seventies–eighties
SCOTTY	a resident aide, twenties–thirties
BENJAMIN, LEWIS and CLOWN	played by the same actor, forties
COLLEEN and WOMAN IN WHITE	played by same actress, thirties–forties
DEREK, ZOMBIE BUTLER and MASKED MAN	played by the same actor, thirties–forties

PLACE

The play is mostly set in a double room at the Bristol Place Senior Living Facility in suburban New Jersey. Though there are a few other locations.

NOTE

A slash (/) in the dialogue indicates the start of the next spoken line.

ACT ONE

SCENE ONE

A double room in the Bristol Place Senior Living Facility. It's fairly homey, as far as these places go. There are two beds, a couple of end tables, two sitting chairs, and two identical dressers. There's a door to the room stage right that leads out into the hall. A wide set of windows line the stage left wall. It's a very sunny day. A door upstage right leads to the bathroom.

As the lights rise, we discover Abby Binder in the chair closest to the windows, reading on an iPad. Her side of the room, stage left, has a few plants and a watering can on the windowsill, and some knickknacks. Her bed is made, while the stage right bed is not. The stage right dresser has several framed family photos atop it, while Abby's dresser has a small stack of books.

There's a tap at the door. Scotty, a resident aide, enters, carrying a tray with a couple of covered plates on it.

SCOTTY

Hey, Abby. You didn't want to come down to the dining room?

ABBY

(Doesn't look up from her iPad) Am I there?

SCOTTY

That's all right, I brought some lunch up for you. *(Places the tray near her)*

ABBY

Why bother? I can't taste anything.

SCOTTY

I know, I'm sorry.

ABBY

Going on two months now. Which may be a blessing given what they serve down there.

SCOTTY

It's very common. Losing your sense of taste.

ABBY

No, it isn't.

SCOTTY

I've seen it with a lot of our residents. It's usually the medications. Certain combinations do funny things.

ABBY

Oh, are you a doctor now?

SCOTTY

No. The plate's right there when you get hungry. It's shrimp marinara.

ABBY

It doesn't matter what it is. It all tastes like sand to me.

SCOTTY

Okay.

(He makes the unmade bed over the following:)

ABBY

How long is that woman here?

SCOTTY

What do you mean?

ABBY

It's been three weeks. And she never stops talking. How long is this supposed to go on?

SCOTTY

This is where she lives, Abby.

ABBY

Well yes, for *now*, but I / meant—

SCOTTY

Not just for now. Indefinitely. This is Marilyn's room. Same as you.

ABBY

But I thought she was being moved as soon as a bed opened up. And from what I hear, that fat woman on the first floor died last night.

SCOTTY

Mrs. Moore. Her name was Mrs. Moore.

ABBY

Well I can't keep track of everyone's name. You knew who I meant. She's dead isn't she?

SCOTTY

She passed away, yes.

ABBY

Then there's an open bed.

SCOTTY

I think Marilyn prefers this room. She said she likes the view of the park. She's very happy in here.

ABBY

But everyone wants the first floor. It's closer to everything. And I've *always* had my own room, Scotty.

SCOTTY

That's not true.

ABBY

Most of the time. That Spanish lady was here for a few months, but after / her—

SCOTTY

If there's space, we try to accommodate you, but there's not always space. And you don't have a private room.

ABBY

Not officially maybe.

SCOTTY

If you and your family want to *pay* for a private room—

ABBY

If I *have* to have someone in here, why can't it be someone quiet? What about that woman without the voice box? She seems nice.

SCOTTY

So is Marilyn. You just need to give her a / chance.

ABBY

That woman is troubled, Scotty. I think there's something wrong with her. She's always trying to make little *bets* with me.

SCOTTY

What do you mean, bets? What kind of bets?

ABBY

Just the stupidest things. Guessing games and quizzes. This morning she wanted to race me to the elevator. Last night she bet me she could balance a slipper on her head.

SCOTTY

Could she?

ABBY

I don't know, I rolled over. You have to get her out of here.

SCOTTY

I can't *force* her to leave, Abby.

ABBY

Management could. Charlie Hastings would've done it. He always made sure I had my own room.

SCOTTY

Well, Charlie doesn't work here anymore.

ABBY

Which is a shame. Charlie liked me.

SCOTTY

I like you too. But, I'm not in charge of room assignments. Miss Larusso is.

                            ABBY

Well you're friends with her, aren't you? I see you in her office
all the time watching those cat videos or whatever they are.
They must be very funny the way you two carry on.

                            SCOTTY

They aren't cat videos.

                            ABBY

No?

                            SCOTTY

Not all of them.

                            ABBY

Can't you talk to her?

                            SCOTTY

You talk to her. Be your own advocate.

                            ABBY

Oh that never works. Besides, Miss Larusso doesn't like me.

                            SCOTTY

Because you're mean to her.

                            ABBY

Her problem is, she has no sense of humor. Charlie Hastings
thought I was hilarious.

                            SCOTTY

Because he was drunk.

                            ABBY

You leave that man alone.

SCOTTY

He had a terrible drinking problem, which is why he was fired.

ABBY

All I know is, he did whatever I asked him to. If he were here, that woman would've been gone by now.

(Marilyn enters. She's warm and pleasant.)

SCOTTY

There she is.

MARILYN

Here I am.

SCOTTY

How you feeling, Marilyn?

MARILYN

I feel *great*, thank you. Just back from my walk.

SCOTTY

Oh, are you doing that now?

MARILYN

Every day after lunch. Twice around the park. Me and Alice and Sally. Mr. Hantz comes along sometimes. I've invited Abby but she doesn't like the exercise.

ABBY

It's not the exercise I don't like.

MARILYN

Did you make my bed, Scotty? I've told you that you don't have to do that. I'm only gonna mess it up again. I'm a restless sleeper.

ABBY

Also she snores.

MARILYN

It's true!

ABBY

I had to get earplugs.

MARILYN

My Oliver used to boot me out of bed. Usually it's the husband on the couch, but with us it was *me*. Poor man.

ABBY

My very thought.

MARILYN

(Chuckles at that) Isn't she awful, Scotty?

SCOTTY

She is, yes. She's awful. *(As he exits)* I'll be back.

MARILYN

We missed you in the dining room. You should see it down there. They have it all done up for Halloween now. Pumpkins up on the walls, skeletons, black cats. You'd love it.

ABBY

Why would you think that?

MARILYN

They're like classroom decorations. And Mr. Hantz said you used to be a teacher. Grade school, he said. I don't know how he got it outta ya, you won't tell *me* anything.

ABBY

(Looks to the windowsill) My plants are droopy.

MARILYN

But teacher makes sense. I can picture it. I bet you were very stern with the children.

(Abby grabs the watering can and heads into the bathroom. We hear the water running.)

I was an office manager. In my husband's business. Did I mention he was a skydiving instructor?

ABBY

Several times.

MARILYN

We were based down at Alexandria Field. I could tell you some stories, boy. My children run the business now. They're good kids. And they'd do *anything* for me.

(Abby comes out of the bathroom with the watering can filled. She waters her plants over the following:)

Did you hear that Mrs. Moore died? Poor thing. Went in her sleep. Such a nice woman.

ABBY

Such a nice *room*.

MARILYN

Room?

ABBY

It's too bad she's dead, but silver linings, right?

MARILYN

How do you mean?

ABBY

That room is prime real estate in this place. First floor—between the mailboxes and the dayroom. Less walking, more space.

MARILYN

Are you thinking of changing rooms?

ABBY

What? No, I'm not thinking of changing rooms.

MARILYN

Oh, you sound so enamored of it.

ABBY

I'm not. I only mentioned it because I thought *you* might want it.

MARILYN

Oh no, I'm perfectly happy where I am. There's much more sunlight up here.

ABBY

No there isn't.

MARILYN

(Moves to the windows) Sure there is, we don't have that building blocking our view like they do downstairs. And I can see the park from up here. There's your bench where you like to sit and read. It's a lovely view.

ABBY

I guess I've never noticed.

MARILYN

Well that's a waste, with you so close to the window. Maybe you'd like to swap beds?

ABBY

I would not.

MARILYN

No, I don't blame you. It's the nicest spot in the room.

(Abby, annoyed, goes back to her iPad, reading. Marilyn smiles, then takes a child's painting from her dresser.)

Did I show you this? My grandson made it for me. Caleb. So sweet. Do you know what it is?

ABBY

A pap smear?

MARILYN

It's a fire truck.

ABBY

I don't see it.

MARILYN

He loves fire trucks. Ambulances too. Anything with a siren. He can hear one from blocks away. He gets this big grin, and flies to the window to see them pass by. They make him so happy.

ABBY

That's creepy.

MARILYN

Creepy?

ABBY

Those sirens are blaring because people are dying.

MARILYN

(Chuckles) Now come / on.

ABBY

They *are*. Or their homes are going up in flames. Or there's a car accident, or some old man has fallen down some stairs. That's what those sirens mean. People in pain.

MARILYN

Caleb doesn't know any of that. It's just a fire truck to him.

ABBY

Well, when you've heard as many sirens as I have . . . They're nothing to be happy about. Is he all right? In the head I mean, or is he a little . . .

MARILYN

What kind of question is that?

ABBY

Well if he's chasing after fire trucks, you have to wonder. *My* son never did that. Normal boys don't do that.

MARILYN

Of course they do. You're just trying to get a rise out of me.

(Pause.)

So you have a son, huh? What's his name?

ABBY

Barbara.

(A moment, then Marilyn turns her attention to Abby's tray of food.)

MARILYN

You should eat. There's cobbler. It's very good.

ABBY

You know I can't taste / anything.

MARILYN

Oh is that still going on?

ABBY

You know it is. *(Looks under the lid)* And I love cobbler.

MARILYN

I know, I'm sorry.

ABBY

I don't think you are. I think you're gloating. I think you're angry I made fun of your grandson's painting. *(Takes a bite of the cobbler)*

MARILYN

Oh, I don't get angry.

(Beat.)

ABBY

You don't get angry.

MARILYN

Not anymore, no. There's really no point. It always leads to an ugly place. And I don't care for ugly places.

(Beat.)

How's the cobbler?

ABBY

Tastes like paste.

MARILYN

It's peach. I remember you mentioning it was your mother's specialty, so I put in a special request.

ABBY

(Shoves it aside) Well it's much too late for peaches. It's a summer fruit.

(Marilyn takes out her sudoku puzzle book and sits on her bed.)

MARILYN

Have you tried these? Sudoku? I do them every day to keep my brain limber. Sudoku. They're from Japan.

ABBY

Yes, I know.

MARILYN

Would you like to try one?

ABBY

No thank you.

(Marilyn looks disappointed. She works on her sudoku. After a couple beats . . .)

What do you mean, you put in a special request?

MARILYN

I talked to Miss Larusso. I said, is there any way to get some peach cobbler on the menu. And she said, I bet we could arrange that, let me talk to the kitchen.

ABBY

You just asked her and she said, no problem.

MARILYN

She's very nice to me.

(Scotty reenters with their medication.)

ABBY

Did you hear that, Scotty? Miss Larusso is very nice to Marilyn.

SCOTTY

Well Marilyn is very nice to Miss Larusso. Funny how that works. *(Gives Marilyn her pills in a paper cup)*

MARILYN

(Referring to her cup of pills) Say, Bartender, can you make mine a double?

SCOTTY

Oh, I think you've had enough, ma'am. I'm afraid I'm gonna have to cut you off.

(They have a little laugh.)

MARILYN

(To Abby) We do that every day.

ABBY

Yes, I know.

(Marilyn swallows her pills down, then hands the cup back to Scotty. He moves over to Abby, and hands her her pills.)

SCOTTY

Here you go.

ABBY

(To Scotty) Talk to Larusso for me. Please. Just put in the request.

MARILYN

What request?

ABBY

Chicken and dumplings. If you can ask for cobbler, I can ask for dumplings. *(Downs her pills)*

MARILYN

Did Scotty show you his card? He's an actor, you know.

ABBY

You're an actor?

SCOTTY

Well, not professional.

ABBY

(Smiles) No?

MARILYN

Give her a card, Scotty.

ABBY

Yes, Scotty, give me a card.

SCOTTY

Sure. Here ya go. *(Gives her a postcard)*

MARILYN

He was handing them out at lunch. It's a postcard for the play he's in.

SCOTTY

It's not a play.

MARILYN

Oh, I misunderstood. I thought it was a play.

ABBY

(Reading from the card) "Beelzebub's Den."

SCOTTY

It's a haunted house.

MARILYN

Well that's even *better* than a play.

SCOTTY

Some friends of mine rent out a warehouse in Pottsville every year, and decorate it, and we get into makeup and costumes. It's pretty scary.

ABBY

Weird thing to invite residents to.

SCOTTY

I thought it'd be fun for everyone to see what I do outside of this place.

ABBY

Does Miss Larusso know you want to give us all heart attacks?

SCOTTY

No one's gonna have a heart attack.

ABBY

It says on the card, "Heart-stopping horror!" *Heart. Stopping.*

MARILYN

I'd like to go.

ABBY

Yes, I think that's a wonderful idea. You *should* go.

MARILYN

I'm gonna!

SCOTTY

Excellent! Thanks, Marilyn. That puts me at thirty-nine!

ABBY

Thirty-nine what?

SCOTTY

Tickets. Me and my buddies need to sell forty each to break even on the cost of that warehouse.

MARILYN

Oh, you have to come, Abby. You'd make it forty!

ABBY

No, I don't think so.

MARILYN

He needs to sell tickets! And we should support Scotty and his dreams.

SCOTTY

It's not exactly a dream, it's just—

MARILYN

All the nice things he does for everyone around here?

ABBY

What nice things?

MARILYN

Making our beds, bringing our pills . . .

ABBY

That's his job. He's not changing your sheets because he's *nice*, he's doing it because that's what he gets *paid* to do.

MARILYN

It's a twelve-dollar ticket. Throw the kid a bone.

ABBY

I will not.

(Beat.)

SCOTTY

And you wonder why people won't do *you* any favors.

ABBY

What favors? Larusso?

SCOTTY

You want me to talk to her for you, and yet—

ABBY

Now wait a minute. Are you saying you'd be more inclined to put in a good word if I went to your spook house?

SCOTTY

All I'm saying is, it would've been a nice gesture. That's all.

ABBY

I didn't realize you were a scratch-my-back kinda guy, Scotty.

SCOTTY

Well you don't really know me, do you.

MARILYN

You know, I'm happy to talk to Larusso if you really want dumplings so badly.

ABBY

No, I want Scotty to do it. He knows the kind I like.

(Beat.)

SCOTTY

I do. And if you're a little nicer I can try to get them for you.

ABBY

Fine. I'll see the damn show.

SCOTTY

Yes! Forty!

(Blackout.)

SCENE TWO

Ominous music, creaking doors, and screams of terror. Lights up on the entrance to Beelzebub's Den. Marilyn and Abby enter. Marilyn already looks spooked. Abby gives her a little nudge forward.

ABBY

Keep walking. Down the hall they said.

MARILYN

Stop pushing me.

ABBY

God, it smells in here, doesn't it? Like cat piss and pot.

(A Zombie Butler in Victorian dress appears.)

ZOMBIE BUTLER

Good evening, weary travelers, and welcome to my master's home.

MARILYN

Thank you.

ZOMBIE BUTLER

Down this hall lies only despair and torture. Dare ye enter?

MARILYN

We dare! We *dare*!

ZOMBIE BUTLER

Very well. *(Screams . . .)* STEP INTO THE MOUTH OF HELL!

ABBY

Oh for god sakes.

(He disappears. The women approach a wall of framed Victorian portraits.)

MARILYN

(Referring to one of the paintings) Oo! Doesn't this one look like Mrs. Moore?

(There is a screech of music as the painting slides open to reveal a horrific screaming Clown in the frame.)

CLOWN *(Screaming)*   MARILYN *(Also screaming)*
BLEEEEEEEEEEEE-   AHHHHHHHHHHH-
HHHHH!   HHHHH!

(Abby didn't even flinch. The Clown giggles and the painting slides back into place. Marilyn tries to catch her breath.)

MARILYN

Oh my lord, my heart is thumping right out of my chest!

ABBY

Well what did you *think* was gonna happen?

MARILYN

(Grabs Abby's hand) Feel it.

ABBY

No.

MARILYN

Feel my heart.

ABBY

I don't want / to.

MARILYN

Feel it!

ABBY

Would you let *go* of me!

(Abby snatches her hand away. The Zombie Butler appears at the end of the hall.)

ZOMBIE BUTLER

This way, weary travelers . . . This way.

(They continue on, and eventually the space opens up into a torture chamber. The spooky music continues over the screams of torture. In the middle of the room is Scotty. He is dressed in old-time prison stripes, and strapped into an electric chair.)

Step in, don't be shy. I'd offer you a seat, but this one seems to be taken.

MARILYN

Oh look, it's Scotty! *(Gives an excited little wave)*

SCOTTY AS PRISONER

(Panic and desperation) Oh, thank god you're here! Kind strangers, have mercy upon me! There's been a terrible mistake. I don't belong here!

ABBY

That makes two of us.

SCOTTY AS PRISONER

Please, they're trying to kill me. You have to stop them. It's not my time! IT'S NOT MY TI—AAAGGGGGHHHH!!!

(The Zombie Butler has thrown a giant lever. Lights flash and spark as volts of electricity shoot through Scotty.)

AAAGGGGGHHHH! NOOOOOOOO! AAAAAGGGGH-HHH!

(The Zombie Butler switches the electricity off, and Scotty slumps in his chair . . .)

This is it then. Never to see the sky again. Nor my home. Nor the people I love . . .

MARILYN

He's very good.

ABBY

Yes, such a nuanced performance.

(Scotty gives Abby a look.)

ZOMBIE BUTLER

Say your good-byes, cretin! *(Throws the switch again)*

SCOTTY AS PRISONER

(As if electricity is running through him) AAAGGHH! NOOOO, I'M NOT READY TO DIIIIIIIII—!

(He dies. The electricity is switched off. Scotty slumps with his eyes closed. Abby chuckles. Marilyn looks traumatized.)

MARILYN

Aren't you scared?

ABBY

No, I don't *get* scared. Certainly not of this nonsense.

(A giggle echoes through the chamber . . .)

VOICE OF THE CLOWN

Teeheeheeheehee!

ZOMBIE BUTLER

Here comes the master's underling. Come to collect the body.

(The giggles get louder, and the Clown creeps into the light of the room.)

VOICE OF THE CLOWN

Teeheeheeheehee!

MARILYN

Oh god, that damn clown. It's so disturbing. Look at him.

CLOWN

Tra-la-la, the master will be pleased. He loves fried food. *(He whips around suddenly to face the women)* And what is this? Some *aged* meat?

ABBY

Rude.

CLOWN

Teeheeheehee!

(The Clown pulls out a chain saw, which roars to life—BZZZZZZZ. Marilyn screams, the Clown cackles.)

ZOMBIE BUTLER

This way, ladies! Escape while you can!

(The women flee the cackling Clown, and find themselves in another corridor. They pass a cemetery scene—maybe the Grim Reaper wanders among the graves.)

MARILYN

What do you mean you don't get scared?

ABBY

Haven't been in years. That's what happens when you live long enough. Things disappear. Just like my taste buds. Just like your anger. Everything goes eventually.

ZOMBIE BUTLER

Don't dawdle, ladies.

MARILYN

I bet I could find something you're scared of.

ABBY

No.

MARILYN

How about this, I try to find something that makes you scared, and *you* try to find something that makes me *angry*. That'd be fun!

ABBY

I'm not betting you, Marilyn!

(They come upon a child's nursery, all gauzy and white. An empty white crib. A rocking horse. A Woman in White sits in a rocking chair, cradling a baby. A toy piano plunks out the notes of a lullaby.)

WOMAN IN WHITE

(Hums a lullaby:)

La-lala-laaaa-la, la-la-la.
La-lala-laaaa-la, la-la-laaa.

MARILYN

(Whispers to Abby) I find that very unsettling.

WOMAN IN WHITE

(To her baby) Shhh. It's all right. I won't let them take you. It's okay, Mama's here, you precious baby boy. Mama's here.

VOICE OF THE CLOWN

Teeheeheehee. I smell plump, succulent newborn for my master.

WOMAN IN WHITE

(Panicked) Oh no, he wants my baby.

MARILYN

The clown wants her baby.

WOMAN IN WHITE

(Turns on the women) You brought him here! You led him to my baby boy! Get out before he—

VOICE OF THE CLOWN

Tra-la-la . . . tra-la-la . . .

WOMAN IN WHITE

Oh no, it's too late! We've been discovered!

VOICE OF THE CLOWN

Pink little toes, and pink little ears . . .

(The Woman in White grabs a large crucifix, and thrusts it at Marilyn.)

WOMAN IN WHITE

You, take this crucifix!

MARILYN

Oh god.

WOMAN IN WHITE

(Then to Abby) And you take my baby.

ABBY

No, thank you, I don't want / to—

WOMAN IN WHITE

(Tosses the baby at her) TAKE HIM! And let no evil come upon him!

(Abby catches the baby. The Woman in White runs, and leaps into the crib to hide. Abby looks down at the baby, oddly intrigued by all of this. The Clown emerges from the shadows.)

CLOWN

Ahh, the nursery. That means there are children about. Come out, come out, wherever you are . . .

MARILYN

He's looking for that baby.

ABBY

I know.

MARILYN

Don't give it to him.

ABBY

I *know*.

CLOWN

(Whips around) Ohhh, if it isn't my *old* friends. And what is that in your arms? Why, it's a wee babe. A morsel for my master!

(He moves in for the baby, and Marilyn holds out the crucifix defiantly.)

MARILYN

BACK!

CLOWN

(Recoils) Nooooo!

MARILYN

BACK you demon clown!

CLOWN

Nooooo! Not the crucifix! The sight of it burns me!

MARILYN

You shall not take this child! Begone!

CLOWN

Agggggggghhh!

MARILYN

Begone, I say!

CLOWN

(Retreating into the shadows) You have repelled me! My master shall hear of this! *(Giggly sobs as he exits)*

WOMAN IN WHITE

(Leaps out of hiding) You did it! You saved my baby! Thank you!

MARILYN

You're welcome.

WOMAN IN WHITE

(Turns to Abby) Please, may I have him back?

(But Abby doesn't move. She's still looking down at the baby, cradling it protectively.)

MARILYN

Abby?

WOMAN IN WHITE

Please, madame. I want my boy.

(A moment, and Abby looks up at them. She reluctantly hands the baby back.)

Ohh, there he is. Nothing will ever harm you. *(Singing her lullaby:)*

La-lala-laaaa-la, la-la-la.
La-lala-laaaa-la, la-la-laaa.

(The Zombie Butler reappears.)

ZOMBIE BUTLER

Let us depart, ladies.

(But Abby is still transfixed by the woman and her baby.)

Next room, madame.

MARILYN

Abby, it's time to go.

(Abby finally heads for the exit.)

WOMAN IN WHITE

La-lala-laaaa-la, la-la-la.
La-lala-laaaa-la, la-la-laaa.

(The lights fade on the Woman in White, rocking her baby.)

SCENE THREE

Lights up on Abby and Marilyn's room. Abby is puttering about anxiously when Scotty lets himself in.

ABBY

Oh good, you're back! I've been on pins and needles all morning. You did it? You talked to Larusso?

SCOTTY

I did.

ABBY

Oh thank god! I *knew* you'd do it. And just in time! I don't think I could've taken another day with that woman. So when is she out?

SCOTTY

She's not.

(Beat.)

ABBY

What?

SCOTTY

Larusso denied your / request.

ABBY

Don't tell me that. Do not say that to me.

SCOTTY

I told you it was a long shot.

ABBY

You explained the situation? How there was an empty bed downstairs / and how—?

SCOTTY

It's a no-go, Abby. I'm sorry.

ABBY

You promised to help me. You said if I went to / your—

SCOTTY

I said I would *try*.

ABBY

Try! Try! Story of my life! Everyone *tries*! And nobody *does*.

SCOTTY

The problem is, Marilyn doesn't want to leave. And Miss Larusso doesn't wanna pull her out of here. What am I supposed to do?

ABBY

Charlie Hastings would've figured it out. He hauled all manner of people out of this room. You clearly don't give a shit.

SCOTTY

Don't say that.

ABBY

You obviously have your favorites, and I'm not one of them.

SCOTTY

I don't pick favorites. I try to treat every resident with the same kindness and respect.

ABBY

Ha!

SCOTTY

You may not believe this, but I actually *want* you to be happy.

ABBY

Well you failed, because I'm not.

SCOTTY

And I'm sorry about that.

ABBY

You're sorry? I'm the one who dragged herself to that asinine spook house for nothing. *(Moves to her watering can)* You're a terrible actor by the way.

(Beat.)

SCOTTY

Did you just say I'm a terrible actor?

> ABBY
> *(Watering her plants)* I'm just being honest. If you go and invite me to something like that, I'm gonna give you my review.

(Beat.)

> SCOTTY
> Right.

> ABBY
> Twelve bucks for that shit show.

> SCOTTY
> You want your money back, Abby?

> ABBY
> That'd be a step in the right direction.

> SCOTTY
> Fine. *(Rummages in his pocket for money)*

> ABBY
> Well don't get upset.

> SCOTTY
> *(Sort of throws a few bills in her direction)* Here, take it. *Take* it!

> ABBY
> If you wanna be a real actor you're gonna need some thicker skin.

> SCOTTY
> Don't tell me what I need to be a real actor. You don't know anything about it.

ABBY

There's only seven / dollars here.

SCOTTY

That's all I have right now! I'll go to the ATM at lunch! *(Turns to leave, but then comes back at her)* But you know . . . for the record, Charlie Hastings did not do you any favors.

ABBY

No?

SCOTTY

No. He was not pulling residents out of this room as a *favor* to you, he was doing it as a favor to *them*.

ABBY

All right, if that makes you feel / better.

SCOTTY

There wasn't a single person placed in this room who didn't want out of it within a week. This may come as a shock, but you're apparently not the easiest person to live with.

ABBY

Hey, I don't know what Charlie had to put in the records / but—

SCOTTY

It's not the records, it's common knowledge. No one wanted to live with you. Charlie got so sick of the room-change requests that he just stopped putting people in here.

(Abby stops watering, and faces him.)

I did my best with Larusso, despite what you may think, but she made it very clear—not only will she *not* eject Marilyn from this room, she said it's my job to *keep* her here, because god knows if Marilyn *does* leave, we may never be able to fill that bed again.

(Silence.)

ABBY

Okay. Thank you for clearing things up.

(Scotty stands there for a moment, already regretting saying all this.)

SCOTTY

Look, I'm sorry—

ABBY

No-no-no, don't do that. Don't be sorry. I *like* the truth. I'm not thin-skinned like you are. You don't need to worry about me.

(Beat.)

SCOTTY

Okay.

ABBY

I do want the rest of that money though.

(He regards her. Then Marilyn enters with a tray. It has a couple of covered plates on it.)

SCOTTY

There she is.

MARILYN

Here I am.

SCOTTY

How was breakfast?

MARILYN

Delicious. They were about to close up the dining room, so I got you a few things, Abby.

SCOTTY

What a sweet lady. I'll be back.

(He exits. Marilyn places the plates on the end table closest to Abby.)

MARILYN

There's some scrambled eggs under this plate, and a little sausage. And this is a waffle. I put the syrup on the side. I know you say it all tastes the same, but I thought I'd give you some options anyway. *(Looks at her)* Everything all right?

ABBY

My request was denied.

MARILYN

No chicken and dumplings then?

ABBY

That was never what I wanted.

MARILYN

No, I didn't think so. I assumed you were trying to get me booted from this room.

(Beat.)

ABBY

You knew.

MARILYN

You're not one for subtlety.

ABBY

Look, some people like having someone around. I'm not one of those people.

> MARILYN

I'm not transferring downstairs.

> ABBY

Well you're gonna have to transfer *somewhere*, because this isn't working out. We're just not a good match. Now I'm sorry if that hurts your feelings—

> MARILYN

It doesn't.

> ABBY

Well . . . good. Then you understand what I'm trying to say.

> MARILYN

I do. But I don't think it's true.

> ABBY

No, it *is*.

> MARILYN

I think we're a fine match.

> ABBY

I don't enjoy your company.

> MARILYN

That's all right. I like the view, and the sunshine. And I don't mind your personality.

> ABBY

I don't like you. It's that's simple. I don't like you, and I want you to go.

> MARILYN

If you're so unhappy, maybe *you* should take Mrs. Moore's bed.

(Beat.)

ABBY

Oh my god, is that what this is? A shakedown? Are you trying to take this room for yourself?

MARILYN

No.

ABBY

Because I have been here four years, and you are not going to displace me! I have *earned* this room, and I am *staying* in it!

MARILYN

Oh good. I'm glad to hear you say that. I prefer you stay as well, but you seemed intent on our not living together.

ABBY

You prefer I stay.

MARILYN

I do.

ABBY

Why?

MARILYN

Because you remind me of my husband.

(Beat.)

ABBY

Oh, lord.

MARILYN

He was all pushback and bluster too. And I got very good at working around that. It's sort of my area of expertise. If I lived with him, I can certainly live with you.

ABBY

Marilyn—

MARILYN

You need to stop. Because I'm not leaving.

(*A stalemate. Neither woman budges. A few moments pass, and then Abby reluctantly has to accept that it's come to this . . .*)

ABBY

What if I took your bet?

(*Beat.*)

MARILYN

My bet?

ABBY

If I win, will you go?

MARILYN

Which bet are you talking about? Balancing the slipper?

ABBY

No, the one you made at the spook house.

MARILYN

Where I try to scare you?

ABBY

If you can do that, then you win. Unless I make you angry first.

MARILYN

Then *you* win.

ABBY

Nice and simple.

(Beat.)

MARILYN

What are the ground rules?

ABBY

Scotty can't know.

MARILYN

Oh, I'd hate to keep a secret from / Scotty.

ABBY

Scotty. Can't. Know. If he does, he'll blab it to Larusso, and she'll shut it down.

(Beat.)

MARILYN

Okay. What else?

ABBY

Just that you agree to leave this room if I win.

MARILYN

And what if *I* win?

ABBY

You get to stay.

MARILYN

But I *already* get to stay. I *live* here. What *more* do I get?

(Beat.)

ABBY

What more do you *want*?

MARILYN

I want the bed by the window.

(Beat.)

ABBY

Okay.

MARILYN

Then I'm in. Bet?

ABBY

Bet.

(Blackout.)

SCENE FOUR

Abby and Marilyn's room. The phone beside Marilyn's bed is off the hook. Abby sits in her chair, reading on her iPad. She is sleepy. Through the open bathroom door, we see Marilyn by the mirror. She's wearing a nice outfit, and is putting on a necklace.

MARILYN

You remember Colleen. You met her when I moved in here. She's my youngest daughter. She and her brothers took over the family business. She was the only girl interested in airplanes! Anyway, she's Caleb's mom. He's the one who likes the fire trucks.

(Abby dozes off.)

And you know what's funny about Caleb? He couldn't say Gramps—this was last year when my Oliver was alive—so he called him Grumps, which we all thought was so funny, because it fit him perfectly. Grumps. *(Finished in the bathroom, she comes into the room)* Isn't that funny?

ABBY

(Her eyes fluttering open) Hm?

MARILYN

I'm sorry, were you sleeping?

ABBY

I just dozed off for a second.

MARILYN

You must be tired from last night. The phone keep you up?

ABBY

Didn't keep *me* up. I have earplugs, remember?

MARILYN

Well I wasn't saying anything important. Just family stuff. *(Puts on a little perfume)* It's amazing though, isn't it? All these people.

ABBY

What people?

MARILYN

The ones I've generated. I still can't get used to it. You have a few kids, and that's all it takes. You raise them, and see them off, and then *your* kids have a few kids, and then all *their* kids have a few kids, and soon you're asking, well, where did all these people come from? And then you remember, oh my lord, they came from *me*. *I* did that. So strange.

ABBY

Yes, it is.

MARILYN

It's like that old shampoo commercial. "They told two friends, then *they* told two friends. And so on and so on."

ABBY

That wasn't the case for me.

MARILYN

No?

ABBY

No.

MARILYN

You had your son though.

ABBY

And that was the end of that.

(Marilyn looks to her, intrigued. Scotty enters with their afternoon medication.)

MARILYN

There he is!

SCOTTY

Here I am! *(Referring to Marilyn's outfit)* You have a date, pretty lady?

(He hands them their meds over the following:)

MARILYN

Colleen and her husband are taking me out for lunch.

SCOTTY

Oh, I'm jealous. I wanna go on a lunch date.

> MARILYN

You should ask Miss Larusso! There's a Chipotle down the street. I bet she'd like that.

> SCOTTY

(A nervous laugh, then . . .) Why is your phone off the hook?

> ABBY

Why don't you put it back and find out?

(A moment. Then Scotty puts the phone back on the hook. The phone immediately starts ringing. Scotty looks to Marilyn.)

> MARILYN

Well, go on.

> SCOTTY

(Answers the phone) Hello? . . . Am I what? . . . Um, I don't think so. *(To Marilyn)* Are you giving away a futon?

> MARILYN

Nope.

> SCOTTY

(Back into phone) No, we're not giving away a futon . . . Sure thing. *(Hangs up)*

> MARILYN

Abby put my phone number on craigslist.

> SCOTTY

She what?

> MARILYN

She posted an ad saying I was leaving the country and wanted to give away my belongings. So now my phone won't stop ringing.

ABBY

I attached a list of items.

MARILYN

Free to whoever wanted them. Furniture, appliances, knickknacks, a car.

SCOTTY

A *car*?

ABBY

Toyota Camry. Only eighty thousand miles on it.

MARILYN

For free. Call Marilyn. With my phone number on the bottom.

(The phone rings again. Marilyn answers.)

Hello? . . . No the crock-pot was claimed, I'm afraid . . . Yes,
but thank you for calling . . . Well I *will* have a nice move, that's
so sweet of you to say. Bye-bye now. *(Hangs up, and unplugs
the phone)* The calls just keep coming. All day yesterday, and
through the night. I had to finally take the dang thing off the
hook.

SCOTTY

You can't do that, Abby. You can't torture her / until she—

MARILYN

Oh it's nothing like that. It was just a gag. Abby knows I love
a gag. She was just trying to make me laugh.

ABBY

It's true. I was trying to make her laugh.

(This confuses Scotty. He looks to Marilyn.)

                           SCOTTY
You weren't angry?

                          MARILYN
Nope. Didn't make me angry at all. I thought it was funny.

                            ABBY
She thought it was funny.

                          MARILYN
And I got to chat with all sorts of lovely people. One man
called himself a hoarder, which I don't believe in, but he was
very nice. And very disappointed I had nothing to give him.

                           SCOTTY
You don't believe in hoarding?

                          MARILYN
No, we never had that. Back in my day we called people pack
rats, but it was never serious. It was kinda quaint actually. "Oh
you ol' pack rat you."

                           SCOTTY
But it's a real thing, Marilyn. Hoarding. It's not quaint, it's an
actual disorder.

                            ABBY
Yes, everything's a disorder now.

                          MARILYN
Well that's just silly to me. Look at my Uncle Joe. He was
a barber, and he'd sweep up the hair every night and take it
home in garbage bags. For years. His house was filled with
the stuff. Big bags of hair piled up to the ceiling. By the end,
he could hardly move from room to room without those bags
tumbling down on top of him. Big avalanche of hair bags.

(Beat.)

SCOTTY

And you don't think he had a disorder?

MARILYN

No. Uncle Joe was just *eccentric*. Why can't people be peculiar anymore? We thought it was *funny*. *(Beat)* Until the fire, of course.

(Scotty and Abby just stare at her. Then Scotty turns back to Abby.)

SCOTTY

Well, I have to say, it's nice you two are finally getting along. But you shouldn't put her phone number on the internet.

ABBY

No, I know, I felt terrible about that. Her family couldn't get through on the line. I'm sorry, Marilyn.

MARILYN

Oh that's all right. *(To Scotty)* Colleen just called the front desk. That's how I found out they were coming. We're going out for Middle Eastern food.

SCOTTY

That'll be nice.

MARILYN

They take care of me. Always have. *(Looks to Abby)* Oh look, she dozed off again. Poor thing can't keep her eyes open.

(Scotty goes to move Abby's iPad, but Abby wakes up and clutches it.)

ABBY

What are you doing?

SCOTTY

You were sleeping, and I didn't want you to drop this.

ABBY

I wasn't sleeping. I don't sleep in the middle of the day.

SCOTTY

Are you feeling all right?

ABBY

I'm fine. Just a little low energy today.

SCOTTY

Did you eat your lunch?

ABBY

Most of it. I couldn't taste / it, but I ate it.

MARILYN

You know what you should do? Whatever they serve, you should pretend it's peach cobbler.

ABBY

Why would I do that?

MARILYN

It's your favorite. Just close your eyes and I bet you start to taste it.

SCOTTY

Sense memory.

MARILYN

Is that what it's called?

SCOTTY

It's an acting trick.

MARILYN

Can you show us, Scotty? How it's done?

ABBY

No, that wouldn't work for me.

MARILYN

Let's try it and see!

ABBY

I don't want to.

MARILYN

All right. She doesn't want to try sense memory, Scotty.

SCOTTY

That's probably for the best. I'm gonna pop in on Mr. Hantz.
I'll be next door if you need me.

(Scotty exits. Abby goes back to her iPad. Marilyn checks her watch.)

MARILYN

They're a little late.

ABBY

Are they?

MARILYN

One o'clock they said.

ABBY

Oh. It's almost one thirty.

MARILYN

Must be traffic.

ABBY

You'd think they'd call and tell you they were running behind.

MARILYN

Well how could they get through, Abby? The phone's unplugged.

ABBY

That's true. They could call the front desk though. That's what they did before, isn't it?

MARILYN

They'll be here.

ABBY

I hope so. You're so looking forward to the visit. Getting all dressed up like that. It'd be a shame if they didn't show.

MARILYN

They will.

ABBY

You sound so sure.

MARILYN

Why wouldn't I be?

ABBY

No reason.

(Abby reads. Marilyn waits.)

MARILYN

They told me they'd be here.

ABBY

Oh, they *told* you.

MARILYN

Yes.

ABBY

Called the front desk, did they?

MARILYN

Colleen did, yes.

ABBY

And you talked to her.

MARILYN

No, she left a message, saying they'd pick me up at one, and Barry at the desk gave it to me.

ABBY

Oh. Barry gave you the message. Then how do you know it was really Colleen who called?

MARILYN

Well who else *would* it be? *(Silence)* Did you leave that message, Abby? *(No response)* Did you pretend to be Colleen and leave that message?

ABBY

"Hi, I'm trying to reach my mother on the third floor, but her phone seems to be on the fritz, could I leave a message with you?"

MARILYN

Is that what you did?

ABBY

No rules, you agreed.

(Beat.)

MARILYN

That was a mean thing to do. Very mean-spirited.

ABBY

Yes it was. Are you angry?

MARILYN

It's a shame you had to stoop to this kind of thing.

ABBY

Seems like you might be angry.

MARILYN

You knew what this would mean to me.

ABBY

Well yeah, that's kinda the point.

MARILYN

There are lots of things you could've done to try and make me angry. This one is pure spite. Spite and envy. Because I have people willing to visit me.

ABBY

Not today, you don't.

MARILYN

It bothers you that I talk about my family.

ABBY

Oh, you picked up on that, did you?

MARILYN

Because you don't have that in your life. Yes, you have a son, allegedly, but in the four years you've been here, no one has seen him pay you a visit. Has *anyone* come to see you?

ABBY

Listen to how angry you are.

MARILYN

This is not anger.

ABBY

That's not healthy, Marilyn. All that bottled-up fury? You gotta let it out.

MARILYN

You didn't make me angry.

ABBY

Now come on. We made a deal, and you need to be fair. I made you mad, so I won the bet.

MARILYN

But you didn't.

ABBY

Marilyn—

MARILYN

Even if you *had* pulled one over on me, I wouldn't be angry. I'd be / disappointed but not—

ABBY

What do you mean *if* I had pulled one over on you? You came in here last night waving that piece of paper around like you had won the lottery. "Look who left a message! Look who's coming to visit!" You've been waiting like a kid at Christmas for them to show up. And now that they're not, you're pissed! Admit it!

MARILYN

I'm not.

ABBY

You're a liar!

(There's a tap at the door, then Derek and Colleen enter, happy to see Marilyn.)

COLLEEN   DEREK

Hey, Mommy! We made it!   Knock knock! Anyone home?

MARILYN

Ohhh, they're here!

(Abby looks confused. Marilyn and her family all hug and greet one another over the following:)

COLLEEN

Sorry we're late. We got stuck at the tollbooth.

DEREK

Colleen got in the E-ZPass lane again.

COLLEEN

I'm such a dodo.

MARILYN

I wasn't worried.

COLLEEN

We had a line of cars behind us.

DEREK

All of them honking and screaming at us.

COLLEEN

People are so rude.

MARILYN

I'm just glad you made it.

COLLEEN

You look so pretty. Doesn't she look pretty, Derek?

DEREK

She's a supermodel.

MARILYN

I wish!

COLLEEN

And you decorated a little! It looks nice in here!

DEREK

So much sun!

MARILYN

There's more on Abby's side, but yeah.

COLLEEN

And look, Caleb's fire truck!

DEREK

Prominently displayed!

MARILYN

Abby thought it was a pap smear.

COLLEEN

Well that's very specific.

DEREK

I'm gonna have to Google that when I get home.

COLLEEN

Hello, Abby. Do you remember us? We helped Mom move in a few weeks ago. I'm Colleen, and this is my husband Derek.

(No response. Abby has shifted from confused to peeved.)

DEREK

She looks upset.

MARILYN

I said she would be.

COLLEEN

Did you see her face though? Priceless!

ABBY

Oh, you're all in on it. How nice.

MARILYN

She's mad. We've made her mad.

COLLEEN

She should take a lesson.

MARILYN

Oh, right. *(To Abby)* Because *you* were supposed to make *me* mad. Not the other / way around.

ABBY

No, I got it. You're all very clever. Now go fuck yourselves.

COLLEEN   DEREK

(Laughing) Oh my goodness!   *(Also laughing)* Hey, now!

MARILYN

Didn't I tell you?!

COLLEEN

You did! She's just like Grumps!

MARILYN

Just like Grumps! *(Back to Abby)* Did you honestly think I wouldn't verify the message?

COLLEEN

She called and I was like, um, no we didn't leave a message for you. But once she explained the bet, I said, you know what, we *should* come down for lunch!

MARILYN

(To Abby) Isn't that wonderful?

COLLEEN

I didn't know *how* Mom would occupy her time in here. But this little bet? *Way* better than bingo!

DEREK

I just worry about something going wrong.

COLLEEN

He's right, you should probably have a safe-word. Do you have a safe-word?

MARILYN

I don't know what that is.

COLLEEN

Ours is "sassafras."

DEREK   MARILYN
Colleen—   Sassafras?

COLLEEN

Actually it's— *(As if gagged and/or choking)* "MAFFAFRAFF!
MAFFAFRAFF!"

ABBY

Well, you got me. My hat is off to you. But if you wanna make
that lunch reservation, you should probably get going.

DEREK

You know what? You should come with us! Do you like Middle Eastern?

COLLEEN

This place is delicious. It's called Falafel-ly Yours.

ABBY

No thank you. I've already eaten.

MARILYN

That's true. She nearly cleaned her plate.

COLLEEN   DEREK
(Knowing) Ohh, did she now.   *(Also knowing)* That's very
                                    good.

MARILYN

You should come anyway. There's gonna be belly dancing!

ABBY

Honestly, I'll be much happier here. I don't get much alone-time these days.

(An awkward silence, then Derek looks to Marilyn, concerned.)

DEREK

How's this supposed to work? You said she'd come with us.

MARILYN

It's okay, we can wait. She'll be asleep soon. She's been dozing off and on for the past hour, so it won't be long. And there are a couple wheelchairs out in the hall. We can just borrow one of those once she's down, and wheel her to the car.

(Silence. Abby stares at Marilyn, confused.)

What.

ABBY

What are you talking about?

MARILYN

You don't make things easy, I'll give you that. The good news is, I love a challenge.

ABBY

Oh Jesus. What'd you do?

MARILYN

Don't worry about that just now.

ABBY

(Gets up, struggling to stay alert) Did you drug me? Is that what you did?

MARILYN

You just need to sit / back down.

ABBY

Did you put something in my food, Marilyn?

COLLEEN

She did! She put something in your food!

DEREK

I am *so* sorry.

ABBY

What was it! What did you give me!

MARILYN

Six Nytol and a Xanax.

COLLEEN

(Disbelief) That's a lot.

DEREK

(Also disbelief) Holy shit.

MARILYN

I ground it up, and sprinkled it on your tuna fish! Couldn't ya taste it?

ABBY

You motherfucker.

MARILYN, COLLEEN AND DEREK

Grumps!

(Abby staggers around the room over the following. She may knock things over in her struggle to stay upright and awake.)

ABBY

You can't *drug* me.

MARILYN

I *had* to. I really want that bed.

ABBY

(To the others) And you're going along with this?

COLLEEN

We're a very competitive family!

MARILYN

I told you, they'd do *anything* for me.

ABBY

This makes you accomplices, you know. Whatever happens, you are aiding and abetting!

(Abby goes to Marilyn's phone to call for help. It takes her a while to realize that the phone is disconnected. She tosses the phone in the wastebasket.)

DEREK

I really didn't wanna do it. But it's impossible to say no to them.

MARILYN

(Referring to Abby) She's just trying to scare you.

COLLEEN

(To Derek) It's a contest, honey. All in good fun. They both agreed.

(Abby, unable to stay awake, tries to get to a bed. She may or may not make it.)

MARILYN

And she's already done much worse than I have. She had people calling me at all hours. That's sleep deprivation. It's a mode of torture, you know. I'm not gonna torture *her*, I'm just gonna give her a scare.

                    COLLEEN

Exactly. Harmless fun.

(Only then do they realize that Abby is out cold.)

                    DEREK

Oh god, she's out.

                    MARILYN

What'd I tell you? She's been fighting it all morning.

                    COLLEEN

I'll grab a wheelchair. *(Exits the room)*

                    DEREK

What do *I* do?

                    MARILYN

You help me with the body.

(They move toward Abby as the lights fade.)

SCENE FIVE

In the transition we hear the deafening roar of an airplane engine rise up. Lewis, a jump instructor, appears in a pool of light, yelling over the sound of the airplane.

LEWIS

HEY AGAIN, FOLKS! I WANTED TO TAKE THIS OPPORTUNITY TO THANK YOU FOR CHOOSING SKY HIGH ADVENTURES FOR YOUR OUTING THIS AFTERNOON, AND TO BRIEFLY TOUCH ON A FEW THINGS AS WE MAKE OUR ASCENT!

JUST A REFRESHER—FOR THOSE OF YOU WHO DON'T KNOW OR CAN'T REMEMBER, MY NAME IS LEWIS, AND I'M HERE TO MAKE SURE YOU'RE SAFE, SECURE AND HAVING A GOOD TIME! THOUGH NOT NECESSARILY IN THAT ORDER!

I'M HAPPY TO REPORT THAT WE'RE EXPECT-
ING CLEAR SKIES AND IDEAL FLYING CONDI-
TIONS TODAY!

NOW THERE ARE A FEW THINGS TO REVIEW
AS WE MAKE THE CLIMB! THE HARNESS THAT
YOU'RE WEARING IS SPECIFICALLY DESIGNED TO
CONNECT YOU TO YOUR INSTRUCTOR, SO YOU
WILL WANT IT TO BE TIGHT AND SECURE!

*(Eventually the lights come up to reveal that we're inside a jump-
plane. Derek is here, behind Abby, attached by a harness. Colleen is
behind Marilyn, also attached by a harness. They're all suited up for
a tandem skydive. As Lewis talks, Abby's eyes flutter open. She looks
around, confused, wondering if maybe she's dreaming.)*

YOU'VE ALSO BEEN OUTFITTED WITH A PAIR
OF GOGGLES, AND A HELMET! THE HELMET IS
EQUIPPED WITH A MIKE, AS WELL AS A TWO-
WAY RADIO THAT WILL ALLOW YOU ALL TO STAY
IN COMMUNICATION DURING YOUR DESCENT!
IN A TANDEM DIVE, YOUR INSTRUCTOR WEARS
THE PARACHUTE PACK ON HIS OR HER BACK,
AND SO LONG AS YOU STAY CONNECTED TO ONE
ANOTHER, YOU HAVE NOTHING TO BE AFRAID OF!
(Referring to Abby) IS SHE GETTING ANY OF THIS?

(Everyone yells over the roar of the plane:)

COLLEEN
SHE'S BEEN IN AND OUT! I THINK SHE'S COMING
TO THOUGH!

MARILYN
ARE YOU AWAKE NOW, ABBY?

(Abby looks at her, still not comprehending what's going on.)

LEWIS

NOW THIS IS VERY IMPORTANT, SO LISTEN UP! YOU WILL JUMP! BECAUSE YOU ARE TWO PEOPLE STRAPPED TOGETHER, YOU WILL BE FALLING MUCH TOO FAST! A SMALL DROGUE CHUTE WILL SLOW YOUR DESCENT! YOU WILL BE FALLING AT A SPEED OF ONE HUNDRED AND TWENTY MILES PER HOUR! YOU WILL FREE-FALL ALMOST FIVE THOUSAND FEET! AT WHICH POINT THE MAIN CHUTE SHOULD OPEN!

MARILYN AND COLLEEN

SHOULD OPEN! *(They chuckle)*

LEWIS

If THE MAIN CHUTE DOES *NOT* OPEN, WHICH IS VERY RARE, YOU WILL CONTINUE TO FREE-FALL FOR ANOTHER THREE THOUSAND FEET. THIS WILL BE HARROWING. BUT THEN A SECOND-ARY RESERVE CHUTE WILL AUTOMATICALLY BE TRIGGERED, AND YOU WILL LAND SAFELY! DO YOU UNDERSTAND, ABBY?

ABBY

NO! WHAT IS THIS? WHO *ARE* YOU?

MARILYN

THAT'S LEWIS, MY OLDEST BOY! HIS BROTHERS JIM AND PETE ARE IN THE COCKPIT! YOU MET THEM ALL ON THE TARMAC!

ABBY

ON THE *TARMAC*? WHAT ARE YOU—? WHERE THE HELL ARE WE?

COLLEEN

IT'S AN AIRPLANE! YOU'RE IN OUR FAMILY'S AIR-PLANE!

ABBY

YOUR FAMILY'S *WHAT*? HOW DID I—? *(Referring to her harness)* WHAT AM I WEARING?

LEWIS

SHE HASN'T BEEN LISTENING AT ALL, MOM! SHE DOESN'T EVEN KNOW WHAT SHE'S WEARING!

DEREK

IT'S A TANDEM HARNESS, ABBY!

ABBY

(Confused) WHO SAID THAT? WHO'S BACK THERE?

DEREK

IT'S DEREK! WE'RE ATTACHED TO EACH OTHER! THIS IS A TANDEM JUMP!

ABBY

WHAT IS GOING ON HERE?!

COLLEEN

WE'RE ALL GONNA SKYDIVE!

ABBY

LIKE HELL WE ARE! LAND THIS THING RIGHT NOW!

MARILYN

ALL RIGHT, IF YOU'RE SCARED WE CAN DO THAT!

ABBY

I'M NOT SCARED!

LEWIS

GLAD TO HEAR IT! OKAY FOLKS, WE'RE JUST ABOUT AT TEN THOUSAND FEET, SO WADDLE ON

OVER TO THE DOOR, AND WE'LL GET READY TO DO THIS!

(They all waddle over to the door. Abby is reluctant and pissed.)

ABBY

WE'RE NOT JUMPING OUT OF THIS PLANE! IT WOULDN'T BE *LEGAL*! YOU'D ALL GET THROWN IN JAIL!

COLLEEN

BUT YOU SIGNED ALL THE WAIVERS BEFORE WE TOOK OFF!

ABBY

WHAT WAIVERS?

LEWIS

(Pulls out documents) LOOK HERE! YOU DON'T HOLD ANY OF US RESPONSIBLE FOR WHATEVER MIGHT HAPPEN TODAY!

ABBY

I DIDN'T SIGN THAT!

COLLEEN

YOU DID! YOU WEREN'T ENTIRELTY CONSCIOUS, BUT YOU *DID* SIGN IT!

LEWIS

YOU'RE GONNA LIKE THIS, ABBY! IT'S JUST LIKE LIFE! YOU GET SHOVED OUT INTO NOTHING-NESS, THEN IT'S A LONG TERRIFYING FREE-FALL TO CERTAIN DEATH! WHICH IS WHY YOU GOTTA PULL THE RIPCORD, BABY! SLOW YOURSELF DOWN AND LOOK AROUND WHILE YOU CAN!

MARILYN

THAT'S BEAUTIFUL, LEWIS!

LEWIS

THANK YOU, MOMMY!

(Lewis throws open the door of the plane. The sound is deafening. They all fight against the force of the wind.)

DEREK

OH MY GOD!

LEWIS

WE'RE OVER THE DROP ZONE!

COLLEEN

ISN'T THIS EXCITING?!

ABBY

YOU PEOPLE ARE LUNATICS!

LEWIS

NOW REMEMBER, CROSS YOUR ARMS OVER YOUR CHEST, LIFT YOUR FEET AND LAY YOUR HEAD BACK!

MARILYN

WE'LL GO FIRST AND SHOW YOU HOW IT'S DONE!

COLLEEN

READY?

MARILYN

GO!

(Colleen and Marilyn lean out the door, then step off, screaming as they fall:)

MARILYN AND COLLEEN

AHHHHHHHHHHHHHHHH!

(. . . And they disappear from sight.)

ABBY

HOLY SHIT! THEY REALLY JUMPED!

DEREK

YOU DON'T HAVE TO DO THIS, ABBY!

ABBY

(Defiant) NO! I WANT TO! JUST DO IT ALREADY! JUMP!

DEREK

HERE WE GO!

(And with that, Derek and Abby leap into nothingness, screaming as they fall:)

ABBY AND DEREK

AHHHHHHHHHHHHHHHH!

LEWIS

SEE YOU AT THE BOTTOM!

(Lewis and the airplane fly off behind them. There is nothing but the sound of rushing wind, as Abby and Derek scream:)

ABBY AND DEREK

AHHHHHHHHHHHHHHHH!

(They free-fall, plummeting to earth.)

AHHHHHHHHHHHHHHHH!

(This goes on for a couple of beats, before Colleen and Marilyn fly in beside them, also free-falling, also screaming. We hear their voices through the mikes in their helmets.)

MARILYN AND COLLEEN

AHHHHHHHHHHHHHHH!

ABBY AND DEREK

AHHHHHHHHHHHHHHH!

MARILYN

ABBY!

(But Abby can't hear her. And her eyes are clenched shut.)

ABBY! OVER HERE!

(With great effort, Abby opens her eyes and looks over at Marilyn.)

YOU'RE AWAKE *NOW* I BET!

ABBY

I HOPE YOUR CHUTE DOESN'T DEPLOY!

MARILYN

WHAT?

ABBY

YOUR CHUTE! I HOPE IT DOESN'T OPEN!

MARILYN

I CAN'T HEAR YOU!

ABBY

YOUR *CHUTE*! YOUR *CHUTE*! I HOPE YOU *DIE*!

MARILYN

YOU HOPE I *DIE*?

ABBY

YES!

MARILYN

YOU'RE *FUNNY*!

COLLEEN

TIME TO DEPLOY!

MARILYN

GO FOR IT!

(Colleen pulls the ripcord, and their chute deploys. She and Marilyn are whipped up.)

MARILYN AND COLLEEN

(Screaming as they disappear) WOAHHHHHHHHHHHH-HHH!

DEREK

OUR TURN! HOLD ON!

(Derek pulls the ripcord. He and Abby are whipped up.)

ABBY AND DEREK

(Screaming as they disappear) WOAHHHHHHHHHHHH-HHH!

(For a moment we see nothing but clouds and sky. And then . . . Abby and Derek, still attached, float gently back in, their parachute keeping them aloft. Abby catches her breath. She looks around, amazed to still be alive.)

DEREK

We're under canopy! I've got the controls, so you can relax now. We'll be on the ground soon enough.

(Beat.)

You did great, Abby. You should be really proud of yourself.

(They float along for a couple of beats. Then Colleen and Marilyn glide in next to them.)

COLLEEN

Why, hello! Fancy meeting you up here!

MARILYN

Wasn't that amazing, Abby?

ABBY

Don't talk to me.

MARILYN

Were you scared? I know *I* was.

COLLEEN

I've done it a hundred times, and I *still* pee a little bit.

ABBY

(To Marilyn) All this trouble. For a *room*.

MARILYN

Was it fun at all?

(Abby doesn't respond. They float along in silence.)

DEREK

Are we done then? Marilyn wins?

ABBY

No. I wasn't scared.

MARILYN

You were thrown out of a plane, Abby.

ABBY

I wasn't scared.

MARILYN

Abby—

ABBY

I wasn't. Scared.

(Beat.)

MARILYN

Okay. But I don't think I can do much better than that.

ABBY

So you forfeit?

MARILYN

Of course not.

ABBY

Good. Because I intend to get you back for this.

(Beat.)

MARILYN

I heard you screaming, there is no way you weren't / scared!

ABBY

Can you stop talking for a little while? I'm trying to enjoy the view.

(Beat.)

MARILYN

(Smiles) Sure.

(They float along in silence, enjoying the view. They slowly descend, as the lights fade.)

ACT TWO

SCENE ONE

Abby and Marilyn's room. Abby is reading on her iPad. After a couple beats, Marilyn enters, energized.

MARILYN

Good walk today. We picked up the pace a bit. You really should come with us some time. Mr. Hantz is always asking after you.

ABBY

Blech. That's all I need, that horn-dog sniffing around.

MARILYN

You're gonna start turning into an old lady if you don't get out of this room and get some fresh air.

ABBY

I go down to my bench every day.

MARILYN

Yeah, to *read*. Forget sitting on a bench, you gotta move your body.

(Marilyn opens her sudoku book, then stops. She frowns.)

Abby—

ABBY

Yes?

MARILYN

You filled in my sudoku.

ABBY

Yes, I know.

MARILYN

But I was in the middle of that puzzle. *(Flips pages)* Wait . . . you filled in the entire book.

ABBY

Did I?

MARILYN

You didn't even do the grids *correctly*. You just wrote in random numbers!

ABBY

I've never been very good with puzzles.

MARILYN

Not nice. You know this is part of my daily routi— *(Suddenly notices)* There are *letters* in some of these boxes! Why would you put letters in sudoku boxes?

ABBY

To send you secret messages.

MARILYN

What secret messages?

(Marilyn looks more closely, realizes, then looks back to Abby again.)

You're disgusting.

(Abby chuckles, amused.)

Is this supposed to make me angry? Scribbling in my sudoku? Well, you've shot yourself in the foot. Without my puzzle book to keep me occupied, I'll have to focus all of my attention on *you.*

ABBY

Which is why I have earplugs. *(Opens her earplug case, then)* What'd you do with my earplugs?

(Scotty charges in, but stops short when he sees Marilyn.)

MARILYN

There he is!

SCOTTY

(Less enthusiasm than usual) Here I am. *(Beat)* I thought you were out walking.

MARILYN

I just got back. Everything all right?

SCOTTY

Yeah, I just . . . needed to talk to Abby about something.

MARILYN

Oh, is it *Brigadoon*?! *(To Abby)* Scotty was telling us all about how he was in *Brigadoon* in high school. He even sang a little bit for us. *(Back to Scotty)* Miss Larusso looked smitten.

SCOTTY

This isn't about *Brigadoon*. Abby doesn't want to hear about *Brigadoon*. She thinks I'm a bad actor.

MARILYN

He's *not* a bad actor. He's a *wonderful* actor. You would've seen that if you had come to that improv class Scotty gave in the day-room yesterday. We learned so much. We did sense memory exercises! Scotty pretended to eat a banana! He's a terrific actor.

SCOTTY

Marilyn, could I talk to Abby alone?

(Beat.)

MARILYN

Is she in trouble?

SCOTTY

She and I are gonna talk about that.

MARILYN

Oh. Well, all right. Maybe I'll visit Mr. Hantz then. *(Turns to go, but then)* Whatever it is, Scotty, go easy on her.

(Marilyn goes. Scotty looks to Abby.)

SCOTTY

I thought you two were getting along.

ABBY

We are. Like gangbusters. We might braid each other's hair tonight.

SCOTTY

What are these?

(He holds out a fistful of Xeroxed pages. Abby looks them over.)

ABBY

Hm. Look like police reports. Oliver Dunne, it says. That's Marilyn's husband, isn't it?

SCOTTY

You know it is.

ABBY

Looks like Grumps had a temper. Where'd you find these?

SCOTTY

They were posted on the bulletin board in the dining room. And on the walls of the dayroom. And in the elevators. Do you know how many people *saw* these, Abby?

ABBY

Did *she*?

SCOTTY

I hope not. I just spent the past hour taking them all down. I should've made *you* do that.

ABBY

Why? I had nothing to do with it.

SCOTTY

Barry saw you on the security cameras.

(Beat.)

ABBY

(Caught) Well you're the one who wanted us to bond.

SCOTTY

This is bonding?

ABBY

We've been playing practical jokes on each other, that's all.

SCOTTY

This is not a joke, Abby. This is humiliating. Her husband's arrest record? Drunk driving reports? Domestic violence?

ABBY

Surprising, right?

SCOTTY

People saw these. Her friends saw these. Why would you do that to her?

(*Marilyn enters, clutching a few of the Xeroxed police reports in her fist. She looks at Abby. Silence.*)

ABBY

Whadaya got there, Marilyn?

SCOTTY

I'm sorry, I thought I got them all down.

ABBY

You must've missed the ones I slipped under Mr. Hantz's door.

SCOTTY

Are you okay?

ABBY

She's fine. (*To Marilyn*) I told him we've been playing practical jokes on each other.

MARILYN

We have. It's been fun.

SCOTTY

Marilyn—

MARILYN

They're not real. She just had them mocked up. To get my goat. Well-played.

ABBY

Thank you.

MARILYN

It's just a goof, Scotty. Wait'll you see what I'm gonna do to *her*.

ABBY

I bet it'll be funny.

MARILYN

It won't be itching powder in the bed sheets, I'll tell ya that.

SCOTTY

Okay, enough. I don't know what's going on between you two, but this has to stop. If you're really looking to do something together, I'll find you a checkerboard. But this— *(Holds up police reports)* —has to stop.

MARILYN

(Simply) Mind your business, Scotty.

(Beat.)

SCOTTY

What?

MARILYN

We're not hurting anyone. We're not children who need to be scolded. Is this a prison?

SCOTTY

Of course not.

MARILYN

No, this is our home, for better or worse, and we're still free to come and go as we please, and do what we like, so unless we're burning down the building, don't tell us what we can and cannot do.

SCOTTY

Marilyn—

MARILYN

We're just having a little fun. Stay out of it.

(Pause.)

SCOTTY

You know what? You two might be a better match than I thought.

(He goes. A couple beats of silence.)

MARILYN

Where did you get these?

ABBY

Online. You can get *anything* online these days.

MARILYN

Police reports?

ABBY

For a small fee. Don't worry, you're clean. I checked.

(Beat.)

Your husband—not so much. I knew it couldn't *all* be sunshine and cupcakes.

MARILYN

Every marriage has its bad spots, I'm sure you had yours.

ABBY

No one got hit, if that's what you're suggesting.

(Pause.)

MARILYN

I wish you hadn't put these up.

ABBY

No, I know. Are you angry?

(Beat.)

MARILYN

No, not angry.

ABBY

I'd be angry. If someone did that to me.

MARILYN

That's the bet. I agreed to it same as you.

ABBY

I wasn't talking about the bet.

(A moment. Then Abby moves to take the police reports from Marilyn. She crumples them up, and tosses them in the wastebasket. Marilyn regards her as the lights fade.)

SCENE TWO

Late afternoon. Abby is in the park, on her bench, reading on her iPad. After a few moments, a man wearing a bunny mask walks over. He looks around, then sits down on the bench next to Abby. A moment. She looks up from her iPad, glances over at the masked man, shakes her head a little, then goes back to reading.

MASKED MAN

Listen to me, this is very important. Don't do anything foolish. Just hand me the iPad.

ABBY

(Beat.)

(Looks at him) Are you talking to *me*?

MASKED MAN

Don't say anything. Just follow my instructions, and we'll both walk away from this. Okay?

(He pulls out a small pistol and discreetly points it at her. Abby glances at it.)

ABBY

What is that? Is that real? Are you *mugging* me?

MASKED MAN

Ma'am, I need you to stay calm. I'm going to gently take the iPad. *(He does)* Good. And now I need you to hand over whatever's in your purse.

ABBY

There's hardly anything *in* the purse. Certainly not enough money to buy drugs.

MASKED MAN

I'm not gonna buy drugs.

ABBY

Yeah, I've heard that before. *(Shoves purse at him)* Here, take it.

MASKED MAN

(Quietly) No, don't do that! Take the purse back!

ABBY

I thought you / wanted—

MASKED MAN

No, if I take your purse it looks like I'm robbing you. We need to just sit here and look normal.

(He crosses his legs and tries to look normal. But he's wearing a bunny mask.)

Okay, now slowly reach into the purse, and pass me the cash like you're giving me a stick of gum.

ABBY

(Rummaging in her purse) This is so stupid. That tablet is the only thing of value I own. My *books* are on there. What am I supposed to do without my books? *Shame* on you.

MASKED MAN

I'm sorry. I am. I'm sure this is very scary for you.

(Beat.)

Is it?

ABBY

(Hands over a few bills) Is it what?

MASKED MAN

Scary. Are you scared right now?

(A moment, and then she realizes. The Masked Man quickly realizes he's overplayed his hand.)

It doesn't matter, forget I asked. *(Puts the pistol away)* Well, I think this is enough money, I'm just gonna—

(He gets up to go, but not in time. Abby has already whipped out pepper spray and maced the eyeholes of the mask.)

MASKED MAN	ABBY
AH-AH-AAAAHHHH! AHHHHHHHHHHHHH!	No, I'm *not* scared! Are *YOU*! Are *YOU* scared, you son of a bitch?!

(The Masked Man whips off the mask—it's Derek. Colleen leaps out of a bush where she's been hiding.)

COLLEEN

(Screaming their safe-word) Sassafras! Sassafras!

DEREK

G'AAAH! SHE MACED ME!

ABBY

You had a gun!

COLLEEN

IT WAS JUST A TOY! *(Calms her husband)* Okay, deep breaths, baby.

DEREK

M'YAAAAAH! MY EYES ARE ON FIRE!

COLLEEN

Rinse 'em out! There's a water fountain over there!

DEREK

WHERE?! *WHERE?!*

COLLEEN

(Pointing off) THERE! THERE!

DEREK

DIDN'T I SAY THIS WAS A TERRIBLE IDEA?!

(Derek rushes off in pain to rinse his eyes. Colleen turns to Abby, who is calmly packing up her money and iPad.)

ABBY

I thought he was a mugger.

COLLEEN

I don't think you did.

ABBY

Hey, don't get mad at me, your mother's the one who put you up to it. *(Faces front, then looks up)* Is that her up there in the window? *(Calls to her)* NICE TRY, MARILYN! BUT IT DIDN'T WORK!

COLLEEN

This has to stop. I thought the bet was funny, but this has gotten *way* out of hand.

ABBY

And whose fault is that?

DEREK

(From off) Oh god, it burns! It BUUUUUURNS!

COLLEEN

Please, just call it off.

ABBY

Why would I do that?

COLLEEN

Because *she* won't. She's too stubborn, and too proud, and she will take whatever you dish out. She's had a lot of practice in that department, believe me. She's not gonna quit, Abby.

ABBY

Then why should I?

COLLEEN

Because she's not well. I don't know how much she's mentioned about her heart condition / but—

ABBY

Oh, come on, she doesn't have a heart / condition.

COLLEEN

She does, and it's pretty serious. That's why she's in this facility. We wanted her somewhere with doctors on staff, god forbid something goes wrong.

ABBY

You let her jump out of a plane!

COLLEEN

That's like riding a bike to her! What / *you're* doing—

ABBY

There's nothing wrong with Marilyn. You're just scamming me to get what you want. You're just like your mother.

COLLEEN

(A sudden fierceness rising up) I swear to god, if something happens to her because of you I am going to sneak into that goddamn room when you're sleeping and hold a fucking pillow over your face! *(Beat. Then quietly to herself)* Sassafras.

(Derek enters, his face and hair soaking wet, his eyes red and puffy.)

DEREK

I'm not doing this anymore. I can't, with the skydiving and the drugging and the mugging—I can't anymore. I'm done.

COLLEEN

I know. We all are, baby. *(Then to Abby)* It's over, right?

(Abby exits without responding.
Colleen leads Derek off in the other direction. As they go:)

Are you okay?

DEREK

Am I okay? I'm blind and in pain! It's our wedding night all over again!

(The lights fade as they exit.)

SCENE THREE

Abby and Marilyn's room. Afternoon. Abby comes in from a walk outside. She takes off her sunglasses, and dabs her face with a Kleenex. She looks to her plants. They need some water. She grabs the watering can and heads for the bathroom. Abby opens the bathroom door, and finds Marilyn hanging from the back of it, motionless, her eyes closed, as if she's hung herself. Abby, completely unfazed, looks up at Marilyn. A moment. Then she moves past her, fills the watering can, comes back into the room, and closes the bathroom door.

    Abby is watering her plants when Scotty enters with their afternoon medication.

SCOTTY

Did I see you out walking with the group today?

ABBY

Why not? I need exercise the same as anyone else.

SCOTTY

No, it's good you're getting out. I was just surprised. I didn't see Marilyn though.

ABBY

No, I know. She apparently had other plans. *(She takes the pills from him)* It's a gossipy little bunch. You should've heard them going on about you and Larusso.

SCOTTY

What? What about us?

ABBY

Nothing too juicy. They were just debating how long it'd take you to get up the nerve to ask her out.

SCOTTY

(Flustered in spite of himself) Oh. That's a weird thing to— There must be way more interesting things to talk ab— Can I get you some water for those pills.

(Beat.)

ABBY

I would love that.

(Abby watches as Scotty heads to the bathroom. He opens the door, and finds Marilyn hanging there. There's a moment of confusion, and then he begins to scream:)

SCOTTY

AHHHHHH! AHHHH-AHHHHHHHHH!

(This goes on for a moment. Then Marilyn's body begins to shake with laughter. Abby, too, is laughing now. Scotty's terror turns to confusion as he looks from Marilyn, eyes now open, to Abby.)

What is . . . what *is* this?

ABBY

That was fantastic.

MARILYN

I'm sorry, Scotty.

SCOTTY

(Realizing he's been duped) Oh for god sakes.

MARILYN

I'm glad it worked on *someone*. Abby gave me nothin'!

SCOTTY

What is the *matter* with you people? You could've really hung yourself, Marilyn!

MARILYN

No, it's a trick harness. Perfectly safe. I bought it online. Help me down, wouldja?

(Scotty goes to Marilyn and struggles to get her down over the following:)

SCOTTY

How did you even manage this?

MARILYN

Mr. Hantz gave me a boost. I didn't expect Abby to go out for a walk though. I've been stuck up here for two hours.

ABBY

(Chuckles) Oh, that's wonderful. You hanging there, waiting for me. This is the best day ever.

SCOTTY

Is there a strap that loosens it?

MARILYN

Yeah, if you reach around the back— Careful, that hurts.

ABBY

Are you okay?

MARILYN

Ow! You're making it tighter, Scotty.

SCOTTY

Sorry.

ABBY

I only ask because your daughter and I talked yesterday after
I maced her husband.

SCOTTY

After you *what*?

ABBY

They're concerned. They said we should call this off. Because
of your heart condition.

MARILYN

I don't have a heart cond— And I don't need them interfering!
They were lying, Abby. To get you to back down. But don't
you dare do it! Especially not *today*! A bet is a bet!

SCOTTY

(*Stops, and steps away from Marilyn*) What do you mean, a bet
is a bet?

(*Beat.*)

ABBY AND MARILYN

Shit.

SCOTTY

Is that what this is? Oh my god. I knew you had *something* going on.

MARILYN

It's a good one Scotty! If I scare her I get the bed by the window! And if she makes me mad—

SCOTTY

Let me guess.

ABBY

Now don't go runnin' to Larusso.

MARILYN

It's almost over anyway.

SCOTTY

You know what? I don't even— You've officially worn me down. This is like some weird S&M relationship. And I'm not gettin' in the middle of it. You obviously *like* whatever this is. So I'm out. Kill each other, I don't care anymore.

(Beat.)

MARILYN

You're still gonna get me down though, right?

SCOTTY

(A frustrated sigh) Unbelievable.

(He goes back to work, getting her down from the harness.)

I should leave you up here.

ABBY

Yes, you *should*!

SCOTTY

And hang *you* right beside her. *(Struggling with the harness)* This isn't working, Marilyn.

MARILYN

It's easier if you close the door. That's what Mr. Hantz did.

(Scotty goes inside the bathroom and closes the door. We hear their voices inside.)

(Inside the bathroom) If you put your foot on the toilet you can get some leverage.

SCOTTY

(Inside the bathroom) Like this?

MARILYN

(Inside the bathroom) Exactly, but release the strap at the same time.

SCOTTY

(Inside the bathroom) How? I only have two hands!

(The struggle inside the bathroom goes on. Abby chuckles. There's a knock at their door.)

ABBY

Come in.

(Benjamin, a bit rough around the edges, enters, carrying a small potted plant. Abby looks up, and lets out a little gasp.)

BENJAMIN

Hello.

ABBY

(More to herself) Oh Jesus.

BENJAMIN

Can I come in?

ABBY

Looks like you just did.

BENJAMIN

Surprised?

ABBY

That's *one* word.

BENJAMIN

I know. It's weird for me too. *(Referring to the plant)* I brought you this.

ABBY

Thank you.

(We hear grunts and sounds of struggle from the bathroom:)

SCOTTY

(Inside the bathroom) Let me get behind you, and try it that way.

MARILYN

(Inside the bathroom) You're not gonna fit.

SCOTTY

(Inside the bathroom) Would you—?

BENJAMIN

(Referring to the bathroom) Is everything okay, in / there?

ABBY

What are you doing here?

BENJAMIN

Your friend called me. Marilyn?

ABBY

She's not my friend.

BENJAMIN

Oh. Well, she somehow got a hold of a number to this old apartment I lived in, and the guy that's living there now passed on the message to me, so I called her back. Because I thought maybe something bad had happened.

ABBY

To me?

BENJAMIN

Well to get a call out of the blue like that.

ABBY

Yes, I know those calls, Benjamin. They're scary, aren't they.

(Beat.)

BENJAMIN

She said you wanted to see me.

ABBY

She was lying.

(Beat.)

BENJAMIN

Oh.

(The bathroom door bangs, and we hear grunts from inside:)

MARILYN

(Inside the bathroom) Almost there. A little closer.

SCOTTY

(Inside the bathroom) Oh god . . .

MARILYN

(Inside the bathroom) Right there! That's it!

BENJAMIN

Are people having sex in there?

ABBY

Yes. This is a filthy place where people have sex in the bathrooms. It's a shame you had to find me here.

(The bathroom door is thrown open. Marilyn and Scotty stagger out, winded and sweaty.)

MARILYN

God, that was more than I bargained for.

SCOTTY

I was starting to worry I couldn't get you off.

(Beat.)

MARILYN

(Notices Benjamin) Oh, hello.

BENJAMIN

Hi.

MARILYN

Wait, are you him? Oh my gosh, you must be him! I'm Marilyn! *(To Scotty)* That's Benjamin! Abby's son!

SCOTTY

Oh.

MARILYN

It wasn't easy tracking him down. I had to go through Miss Larusso's files while she was at lunch. Were you surprised, Abby?

BENJAMIN

You said she wanted to see me.

MARILYN

I did. I did say that, yes. And I'm pretty sure she does.

ABBY

No, I don't.

MARILYN

She'll come around though. It just takes her a while to warm up. But you probably already know that.

BENJAMIN

I should go.

MARILYN

No, don't do that. You haven't seen each other in five years. Isn't that what you said on the phone? Five years is too long.

SCOTTY

Marilyn.

MARILYN

I'm sure this is bringing up a lot of emotions for / both of you—

ABBY

Oh, for god sakes.

MARILYN

—which can be really scary, I / know.

ABBY

Nobody's scared. Why would I be scared of my own son?

SCOTTY

We should go.

ABBY

Is this my punishment? For those arrest reports?

MARILYN

It's not punishment, Abby. He's your *family*, and / I thought—

SCOTTY

(Firmly) Let's *go*, Marilyn.

(Beat.)

MARILYN

Scotty's right, we should let you two talk. *(To Benjamin)* I'm glad you're here. Stay a while.

(They exit. Benjamin and Abby are silent for a few beats.)

BENJAMIN

I didn't realize she was sick.

ABBY

In the head, you mean? Oh, she's not sick. She's diabolical.

BENJAMIN

She seems so sweet.

ABBY

That's what makes her so diabolical.

BENJAMIN

(After a moment, he looks around) So this is nice. It's a nice place. I would've come to visit sooner, but I had no idea where you were.

ABBY

Well, I wanted to leave a forwarding address, but you were otherwise engaged.

(Beat.)

BENJAMIN

You look good.

ABBY

I *am* good.

BENJAMIN

Me too. Much better than I was. And I'm working. Odd jobs mostly. Dry-walling and things like that. Nothing big, but it pays the rent. I think you'd be proud.

ABBY

Where are you living?

BENJAMIN

In Freehold. With Zoe.

ABBY

I don't know who that is.

BENJAMIN

No, I know. She's, uh . . . pretty great actually. You'd like her.

ABBY

Well I hope it sticks, because if it doesn't work out in Freehold you can't live here. Too many people in this room as it is.

BENJAMIN

I know, Mom.

ABBY

I wanted a private room but there wasn't enough money for that. Actually I wanted to stay in my own house, but it was hard to make those payments with an empty bank / account.

BENJAMIN

Okay, you don't need / to—

ABBY

Are you clean, Benjamin?

(Beat.)

BENJAMIN

Yeah. Almost two years now.

ABBY

Well that's good. If you are in fact / clean.

BENJAMIN

I *am*, Mom.

ABBY

Good. That's good. But you'll forgive me for not patting you on the back. If that's what you came for, then you're out / of luck.

BENJAMIN

That's not what I came for.

ABBY

No? "I think you'd be proud."

BENJAMIN

Are you not?

ABBY

I *was* proud, Benny. The first time you got clean. And the second time and the tenth, and after twenty years of you saying, you're clean, it gets a little hard to muster an "atta boy, kiddo."

BENJAMIN

I bet.

ABBY

But congrats, you're not sticking needles in your arm. Neither am I. Neither is anyone else in this building, except maybe the diabetics. And yet nobody's proud of us. Not for being clean. Because, guess what? You *should* be clean. You *should* be.

BENJAMIN

You're right.

ABBY

I know I am.

(Pause.)

But you're doing better.

BENJAMIN

Yes. Much.

ABBY

So you'll be able to pay me back then?

(No response.)

So not *that* much better. Can I safely assume you didn't meet this Zoe woman on the floor of the New York Stock Exchange then?

BENJAMIN

No, I didn't meet her on the floor of the New York Stock Exchange.

ABBY

But on *some* kind of floor, I bet.

BENJAMIN

(Chuckles) You just let me know when you're finished getting in your punches.

ABBY

Oh it's gonna be a while I think.

BENJAMIN

Then I should probably sit down.

ABBY

What do you want here, Benny?

BENJAMIN

I don't want anything. Your friend / called *me*.

ABBY

She's not my friend.

BENJAMIN

Well, regardless, I'm here. We might as well catch up.

ABBY

Right. I remember how this scene goes now. You come to catch up, and the next day I notice that things are missing.

BENJAMIN

I'm not gonna / take anything.

ABBY

Jewelry, radios, the *change jar*.

BENJAMIN

Jesus. When did you get so mean?

ABBY

Oh it just happened, in dribs and drabs.

BENJAMIN

Because of me?

ABBY

I didn't say that.

BENJAMIN

It's what you think though. All the bad stuff that / happened—

ABBY

Don't tell me what / I think.

BENJAMIN

Daddy, and the house, and you getting fired. It was all my fault.

ABBY

No, that's not what I think. Maybe that's what *you* think, but it's not what I think. The bad stuff wasn't all your fault. *(Beat)* Just *mostly*.

(Beat.)

BENJAMIN

That's fair.

(Silence. A momentary truce.)

ABBY

Marilyn and I have a bet, by the way. That's why you're here. If she scares me, she gets the bed by the window. So she broke into an office, stole my file, and dragged you here hoping I'd flinch.

(Beat.)

BENJAMIN

That's kinda nuts.

ABBY

You have no idea.

(A nice moment between them. But then:)

I think you should probably go.

(Beat.)

BENJAMIN

I don't wanna go.

ABBY

Why not?

BENJAMIN

I just . . . wanna spend a little time with you. Is that crazy?

ABBY

No, not crazy at all. We all *want* things. I certainly did. I wanted to stay in my house, I wanted a healthy son—

BENJAMIN

Would you stop?

ABBY

I wanted holidays and neighbors and barbecues and a garden—

BENJAMIN

You had that. Don't pretend you never had that.

ABBY

Well I wanted *more* of it. I wanted it to keep going. It does for most people / after all.

BENJAMIN

I know. I know / it does.

ABBY

I wanted to get old with Daddy, and take trips to Hawaii, and go to your wedding, and *grandchildren* that I could *squeeze*, and *spoil*. I wanted a *lot of things*, Benny. So no, it's not crazy to *want* to spend time with me. I spent years *wishing* you would want that. But you seemed to want other things more. And now it's too late.

BENJAMIN

Don't say that.

ABBY

Why not?

BENJAMIN

Because I'm here.

ABBY

For now. But you'll go away again. You always do.

BENJAMIN

I won't / this time.

ABBY

Which is what you always say. And I know you *mean* it when
you say it. But then you slip, you can't help it.

BENJAMIN

Well I'd love to give you a *guarantee* / but I can't.

ABBY

That's my point, you *can't*. And I'm too tired to be disappointed again. It hurts too much when it doesn't work out.
And it seems to never work out.

(Pause.)

BENJAMIN

So you're done then. The store's closed. You're gonna spend
the rest of your life in this room stewing about / all the things—

ABBY

Stewing? I'll have you know, I have a very active and satisfying
life here. There are activities and trips and walking groups—
And I jumped out of a plane last week! Well maybe *jumped*
isn't the right word, but / still.

BENJAMIN

What are you talking about?

ABBY

It doesn't matter, the point is, don't wag your finger at me and tell me that I'm done. I'm *not* done.

BENJAMIN

You're just done with *me*.

ABBY

Don't. I have put in my time with you. I have done more than my fair share of parental duty. I don't owe you any more.

(Beat.)

I'd like you to go now.

(Beat.)

BENJAMIN

All right.

(Benjamin pulls a photo from his pocket. Abby doesn't look at him.)

Can I give you something before I do?

ABBY

I prefer you didn't.

BENJAMIN

Mom—

ABBY

Benny, please. Just . . . leave.

(This is more effortful than cold. Abby, whether we see it or not, is trying to hold it together.)

BENJAMIN

Okay. *(Puts the photo back in his pocket)* Your friend has the number at Zoe's if you wanna reach me.

ABBY

She's not my friend.

BENJAMIN

No, I know.

(Benjamin regards his mother, then exits.
After he goes, Abby takes a few moments to collect herself.
After a while, Marilyn reenters.)

MARILYN

He didn't stay long.

(No response.)

Is he coming back?

ABBY

No, I don't think he is.

(Silence.)

MARILYN

Look, Abby, I didn't mean to make trouble.

ABBY

Right.

MARILYN

I knew you might be upset, but I like to think that I was also doing something *nice* for you. He's your only child after all / and—

ABBY

Is there something wrong with you?

MARILYN

I'm sorry?

ABBY

I knew you were odd, but now I realize there might actually be something *wrong* with you.

MARILYN

You're mad at me.

ABBY

To pull *family* into this—?

MARILYN

Now wait a second, *you* did that first. You pulled family into it *first*. The police records, and calling up pretending to be my / daughter—

ABBY

Pretended! I didn't actually *bring* your family here!

MARILYN

But they came!

ABBY

Because you *told* them to! You asked for their help! You drugged me and got / them to—

MARILYN

Only because you started it! You made it personal the minute you ridiculed Caleb's painting.

ABBY

You tracked down my *estranged son*!

MARILYN

I thought it would make you happy. I thought if you saw how well he was / doing—

ABBY

Then *what*, Marilyn?! I'd see the light, and my heart would grow three sizes today?

MARILYN

I think one size would've been plenty.

ABBY

Don't do that. I'm not the mean one here, *you* are, so don't try to flip this around and pretend that you were trying to do me a *favor*.

MARILYN

I was!

ABBY

You might have everyone else fooled, but I see who you are. Flitting around here, rubbing my face in your happiness. Bragging about your children when you know damn well it's a sore spot / for me.

MARILYN

I did *not* know that! How could I? You refused to tell me anything about your family!

ABBY

How lucky, your kids visit, and take you to lunch, and paint pictures! *(Grabs Caleb's painting)*

MARILYN

(Referring to the painting) Be careful with that.

ABBY

(Holds it up) This? *(Pretends to bobble it)* Whoooa-ohhh.

MARILYN

Gimme that painting, Abby.

ABBY

(Moves away from her) No, I don't think I will.

MARILYN

You're obviously mad that I won, but you don't need to lash / out at—

ABBY

You didn't win. I was surprised to see him, but I wasn't scared.

MARILYN

Yes, you were.

ABBY

Of Benjamin?

MARILYN

I could see it on your face!

ABBY

I think someone's finally getting angry.

MARILYN

BECAUSE YOU'RE A CHEATER!

ABBY

(*Chuckles*) Look at you.

MARILYN

ADMIT YOU WERE SCARED!

ABBY

ADMIT THAT YOU'RE ANGRY!

MARILYN

PUT THE PAINTING DOWN!

ABBY

OR WHAT?

MARILYN

Abby—!

(*Rip! Abby has torn the painting in half. She does it again and again. It's in pieces.*
    Silence.)

Okay.

ABBY

Okay?

MARILYN

We're done.

ABBY

Are you angry?

MARILYN

I am. Congratulations. You win.

ABBY

Seriously? That's all it took? If I had known that, I would've ripped up that stupid painting a long time ago.

MARILYN

Maybe I made a mistake bringing Benjamin / here—

ABBY

Maybe?

MARILYN

—but despite what you think, there *was* kindness in it. What you just did was the opposite.

ABBY

Gimme a break. It's a finger painting. He'll make you another one. He'll make you a hundred of them if you want.

MARILYN

That's not the point.

(Marilyn begins to gather up a change of clothes and some toiletries.)

I'm going downstairs. I'm sure Charlene won't mind if I sleep in Mrs. Moore's bed.

ABBY

It's *your* bed now.

MARILYN

(Grabbing clothes) Well done, you got what you wanted. You've chased me off, just like you've chased off everyone else who dared to walk in here. Just like you chased off Benjamin.

ABBY

Good-bye, Marilyn.

MARILYN

(*Grabbing more clothes*) You've hit some bumps in your life. I know you have. More than most. But still.

ABBY

Still what?

MARILYN

You can't give up on people. Once you do, it's all over.

(*Beat.*)

Benjamin asked me to give this to you by the way. (*Hands her the photo*)

ABBY

(*Looks down at the photo*) When?

MARILYN

Just now, when he left. He said you refused to take it.

ABBY

I don't even know what it is.

MARILYN

It's a baby photo, Abby.

ABBY

(*Flips photo over and reads*) "Gideon," it says. Who's Gideon?

MARILYN

Your grandson. He was born three weeks ago. Congratulations.

(Everything stops. Abby looks from Marilyn to the photo, trying to process this. Marilyn grabs her pillow and blanket.)

I'll get the rest of my stuff later.

ABBY
(Referring to the photo) Benny didn't tell me.

MARILYN
Sounds like you wouldn't let him.

ABBY
You'd think it'd be the first thing he'd mention.

MARILYN
Maybe he was trying to ease into it.

ABBY
Benjamin never eases into anything. He's a very abrupt person.

MARILYN
Yeah, well, people change.

(And with that, Marilyn exits. Abby stares down at the photo as the lights fade.)

SCENE FOUR

Abby and Marilyn's room. The next day. Scotty, Colleen and Derek are packing Marilyn's clothes and belongings into boxes. This goes on for a few beats, before Abby enters carrying a shopping bag from a baby clothes store.

ABBY

Oh, hello. *(Crosses to her side of the room)* All hands on deck, I see.

COLLEEN

(To Derek) Would you pass me those photos?

DEREK

Sure. Here ya go.

(He passes her the framed photos. She packs them. The mood among them is a sad and quiet one.)

(Holds up some slippers) What about these?

Yeah, we don't wanna leave anything behind.

ABBY

Clearing out then?

COLLEEN

Almost done. You'll have the place to yourself soon enough.

ABBY

Well there's no hurry.

COLLEEN

No?

(A moment between them. Then Colleen goes back to packing.)

DEREK

This box is good to go.

COLLEEN

This one too. *(To Scotty)* We're just gonna bring these down, and come back for the rest.

SCOTTY

I'll finish up.

COLLEEN

Thanks, Scotty.

(They exit with boxes. Scotty continues to pack up Marilyn's things. Abby empties her shopping bag onto her bed—baby clothes, mostly onesies.)

SCOTTY

You were out early.

> ABBY

Yeah, I wanted to get a jump on things.

> SCOTTY

I brought your lunch up.

> ABBY

Oh good. I'm famished. I ran out of here without grabbing breakfast. *(Referring to the boxes)* I didn't realize she'd be packing up so soon.

> SCOTTY

Marilyn?

> ABBY

Guess she's eager to get outta here.

(Beat.)

Did she mention our fight?

> SCOTTY

No . . .

> ABBY

Well, it doesn't matter. She'll be happier downstairs anyway.

> SCOTTY

She's not going downstairs.

> ABBY

Did another room open up?

> SCOTTY

No.

ABBY

Oh. Then where is she going?

SCOTTY

She's not going anywhere. *(Off her confused look)* Marilyn passed away last night.

(Beat.)

ABBY

What?

SCOTTY

She died in her sleep. Charlene found her this morning.

(Beat.)

I'm surprised no one's told you.

ABBY

But . . . she said the heart condition / wasn't real.

SCOTTY

Yeah, she lied about that.

(Beat.)

ABBY

Oh.

SCOTTY

That's why we're packing up her things.

ABBY

I see.

(Beat.)

SCOTTY

It's not your fault. You know how it is around here. Not every-one wakes up in the morning. *(Trying to keep it together)* She was a good one though. So sweet.

(He goes back to packing. After a couple moments he looks over at Abby.)

You all right?

ABBY

I was gonna show her the onesies I picked out. I mean, I know she was mad at me, but I thought, she'll cool off, and I'll show her these little onesies I bought for Gideon.

(Beat.)

SCOTTY

Who's Gideon?

ABBY

My grandson.

SCOTTY

Oh. Well that would've been nice.

ABBY

Yeah. But she's not coming back.

(Beat.)

SCOTTY

No.

ABBY

Okay.

SCOTTY

I should go give Mr. Hantz his medication. I'll be back in a minute. You gonna be okay?

(Beat.)

ABBY

Yeah. You go ahead.

(Scotty exits. Abby is left alone. She looks around the room, which suddenly feels very empty. And in that moment, the fear creeps in. A few beats pass, and suddenly the bathroom door is thrown open to reveal Marilyn.)

MARILYN

(Yells) Haha!

ABBY

(Lets out a scream) AHHHHHHHHHHHHHHHHHHHH!

(Scotty, Colleen and Derek all burst back into the room.)

SCOTTY

There she is!

MARILYN

Here I am!

COLLEEN AND DEREK

Surprise!

MARILYN

(To Abby) I got you! I-got-you-I-got-you-I-got-you!

ABBY

(Catching her breath) What the *fuck*!

MARILYN

Look at her! You're all my witnesses! She was scared!

SCOTTY

She was definitely scared.

DEREK

Terrified.

COLLEEN

It was a thing of beauty.

SCOTTY

You scared her *twice* actually!

MARILYN

Did I?

SCOTTY

First she was scared you were dead! Then she was scared when you *weren't*!

COLLEEN

That's a two-fer!

MARILYN

I got her! I-got-her-I-got-her-I-got-her! Oh god, it feels so good!

DEREK

We're done, right?

COLLEEN

All done. For real this time.

DEREK

Oh that makes me so happy.

MARILYN

Thanks for your help, Scotty.

SCOTTY

Well, I had to do *something*. I'm glad it worked out. Now if you'll excuse me, I have a lunch date. With Miss Larusso.

MARILYN

Ohhh, isn't that nice?

ABBY

You lied to me, Scotty.

SCOTTY

Sorry about that.

ABBY

You said she was dead.

SCOTTY

I know. And you believed me.

ABBY

Yes.

SCOTTY

BECAUSE I AM A GOOD ACTOR!

(Scotty exits.)

COLLEEN

We should take off too.

DEREK

Mr. Hantz is babysitting.

COLLEEN

That was awesome though. And I got the whole thing on video. *(Pulls out an iPhone from one of Abby's plants)*

DEREK

(Hugs Marilyn) Bye, beautiful.

MARILYN

I'll see you guys this weekend.

COLLEEN

Bye, Abby. *(Hugs Marilyn)* Love you, Mommy. *(Referring to the iPhone recording)* I can't wait to post this on Facebook!

(Colleen and Derek exit. Marilyn turns back to Abby.)

MARILYN

I *knew* I could do it! He said I was dead, and you *believed* him. You were scared, right? Scared I was dead?

(Beat.)

ABBY

I was actually.

MARILYN

Oh my gosh, I thought you might cry. It was so sweet!

ABBY

But the bet was over.

MARILYN

I don't care about the bet! I'm too touched to care! You can have the room! The satisfaction is worth more!

ABBY

No, Marilyn. You won.

MARILYN

No, that didn't count.

ABBY

I mean, before this. With Benjamin. I lied when I said I wasn't scared.

MARILYN

Good, because I lied about the sudoku. That really pissed me off.

ABBY

I know.

MARILYN

You knew?

ABBY

It's okay, because I was shitting bricks during that skydive.

(Silence. Now what? Marilyn notices the onesies.)

MARILYN

Baby clothes?

ABBY

Cute right?

MARILYN

Adorable. So you're gonna see them then.

ABBY

I need to squeeze that baby. *(Looks to her)* I'm glad you're not dead.

MARILYN

Me too.

ABBY

(After a moment) I'm sorry I ripped / the painting.

MARILYN

Water under the bridge. And you were right, I talked to Caleb this morning and he's already painted me three more. Besides, I shouldn't have called / Benjamin.

ABBY

Let's not do this.

MARILYN

Okay.

(Beat.)

You have a grandson!

ABBY

I know!

MARILYN

And a daughter-in-law?

(Beat.)

ABBY

I'm not sure.

134

MARILYN

They're probably not / married.

ABBY

No I don't imagine so. But that's okay. Benny's in a good place. For now. Which . . . I'll take.

(Pause.)

MARILYN

So . . . did I win then, or . . .

ABBY

Let's just call it a draw. You can stay. But I keep the bed by the window.

(Beat.)

MARILYN

Huh.

ABBY

(Turns her attention to her lunch) I have to eat, or I'm gonna pass out. *(Lifts the tray lid)* Oh god, what is that, shepherd's pie? Not that it matters.

MARILYN

I want the bed by the window, Abby.

ABBY

(Looks at her) I'm sorry?

MARILYN

Let's do double or nothing.

ABBY

Now don't start. We finally / settled—

MARILYN

If I win I get the bed, if you win I won't talk before breakfast.

(Pause.)

ABBY

What's the bet?

MARILYN

The one you turned down. The sense memory thing. I'm gonna make that shepherd's pie taste like cobbler.

(Beat.)

ABBY

Okay. *(Reaches for a spoon)*

MARILYN

No-no, put the spoon down. We have to do this properly. Like Scotty taught me. Sit back and close your eyes.

ABBY

(She reluctantly does) Is this gonna take long? Because I'm / about to—

MARILYN

Shhh. I want you to imagine a summer morning. Your mother's in the kitchen just back from the farmer's market.

ABBY

We didn't have a farmer's market.

MARILYN

The supermarket then. She's just back from the supermarket, where she's picked up a basket of peaches—soft, bulging with juice.

ABBY

Sexy.

MARILYN

You're in the kitchen, and you're eight years old, and you watch as she peels and slices the peaches, and tosses them in a saucepan.

ABBY

With the sugar?

MARILYN

Yes, lots of sugar, a little flour, some butter. And she cooks it all up, until it bubbles up and gets syrupy.

ABBY

(Starting to enjoy this) Okay.

MARILYN

And then she pours it all into the deep baking dish, and drops scoops of buttery biscuit dough all over the top, and she slips it into the oven, and you wait.

ABBY

(Inhales) But I can smell it cooking.

MARILYN

Yes, sweet and sticky, and finally it comes out of the oven.

ABBY

And she scoops some into a bowl for me.

MARILYN

She does. Then she smiles and adds a dollop of vanilla ice cream on top. And she hands you the bowl.

(Marilyn hands Abby the bowl with a spoon in it.)

ABBY

And I take a bite?

MARILYN

And you take a bite.

(Abby, eyes still closed, scoops up a spoonful of the food in front of her, and takes a bite. We watch as her face changes over the following:)

And the peaches are so sweet and hot, and the biscuit crust is flaky, and all of that mixed with the vanilla ice cream is maybe the most perfect thing you've ever tasted.

(Abby's face is pure bliss as she chews.)

Can you taste it?

(A long beat.)

ABBY

I can.

(Abby savors the taste, her eyes still closed. Marilyn looks to the bed by the window, as the lights slowly fade.)

END OF PLAY

DAVID LINDSAY-ABAIRE is a Pulitzer Prize–winning playwright, screenwriter, lyricist, and librettist. His play *Good People* premiered on Broadway, was awarded the New York Drama Critics' Circle Award for Best Play, the Horton Foote Prize, the Edgerton Foundation New Play Award, and two Tony nominations. His previous play *Rabbit Hole* received the Pulitzer Prize for Drama, five Tony nominations, and the Spirit of America Award. David also wrote the book and lyrics for *Shrek the Musical*, which was nominated for eight Tonys, four Oliviers, a Grammy, and earned David the Ed Kleban Award as America's most promising musical theater lyricist. David's other plays include *Ripcord, Fuddy Meers, Kimberly Akimbo, Wonder of the World*, and *A Devil Inside*, among others. In addition to his work in theater, David's screen credits include his film adaptation of *Rabbit Hole*, Dreamworks' *Rise of the Guardians*, and *The Family Fang*, starring Nicole Kidman, Christopher Walken, and Jason Bateman. He is Co-Chair of the playwriting program at Juilliard.